AFRICAN AMERICAN
WOMEN
PIONEERS IN STEM

AFRICAN AMERICAN WOMEN PIONEERS IN STEM

T.M. Moody

African American Women Pioneers in STEM
African American History for Kids, #2

Copyright © 2022 T.M. Moody

All rights reserved. No part of this book may be reproduced or transmitted in any form or by any means without written permission of the publisher. For questions, contact us at info@thekulturekidz.com or visit our website at thekulturekidz.com for printables already designated for noncommercial use.

Paperback ISBN: 979-8436050331

Kulture Kidz Books
Tymm Publishing LLC
www.tymmpublishing.com

Author: T.M. Moody
Editor: editorsylvia
Illustrations: johangerrar
Cover and Interior Designer: TywebbinCreations.com

This book is dedicated to future female leaders in STEM!

TABLE OF CONTENTS

Introduction	3
Part 1: Aeronautics	7
Black Female Pilots	7
Bessie Coleman	9
Janet Harmon Bragg	13
Willa B. Brown	17
Timeline	21
More Women to Know!	23
Astronauts & Engineers	27
Dr. Mae C. Jemison	29
Stephanie D. Wilson	33
Dr. Aprille Ericsson-Jackson	37
Timeline	41
More Women to Know!	43
Part 2: Computer Science	47
Human Computers	47
Mary Jackson	49
Katherine Johnson	53
Dorothy Vaughan	57
Timeline	61
More Women to Know!	63

Technology 65

Marsha Rhea Williams 67

Marian Rogers Croak 69

Lisa Gelobter 73

Timeline 77

More Women to Know! 79

Part 3: Health Science 85

Pioneers 85

Mary Eliza Mahoney, RN 87

Dr. Susan McKinney Steward 91

Dr. Ida Gray Nelson Rollins 95

Dr. Ella Phillips Stewart 97

Timeline 101

More Women To Know! 103

Modern Medicine 105

Dr. Marie M. Daly 107

Dr. Patricia Bath 111

Timeline 115

More Women to Know! 116

Glossary 119

Activity Book 125

About the Author 129

Kulture Kidz Books 131

INTRODUCTION

Are your favorite subjects in school math and/or science? Do you like computers? Have you ever thought about learning how to code?

In this book, you will read about African American women who were pioneers in STEM. STEM stands for **s**cience, **t**echnology, **e**ngineering and **m**ath.

The book is split into three major industries or fields that are considered some of the fastest-growing industries, and workers will be needed in the future.

Aeronautics - Aeronautics include careers in aviation, aerospace, and astronautics. Some of the careers may include anything from being a pilot, designing an aircraft, or monitoring flight logistics.

Computer Science - Computer Science is the science and study of computers, including how they are made and how they work. Some of the careers may include designing or developing software, applications, websites and more.

Health Science - Health Science is the study of health, disease and healthcare. People in this industry can be physicians, surgeons, nurses, dentists, medical lab technicians, researchers, and more.

At the end each section is a **Timeline** and **More Women to Know**. A glossary and a bibliography can be found at the end of the book for further research.

NOTE: **This book has a companion activity book. Be on the lookout for how you can get your copy later in this book.**

PART 1
AERONAUTICS

Part 1: Aeronautics

Black Female Pilots

Have you been on an airplane? Are you interested in learning how to fly an airplane? Did you know less than 1% of the world's pilots are African American women?

Let's learn about African American women who were pioneers in aviation.

BESSIE COLEMAN

1892 – 1926

Bessie Coleman was the first African American female and Native American female pilot.

Bessie Coleman was born on January 26, 1892, to a large family of 12 siblings in Atlanta, Texas. Her mother worked as a maid, and her father, who was part Native American, worked as a sharecropper. **Sharecropping** was a hard life where farmers had to give the landowner a portion of their crop.

Bessie always had a strong desire to better herself. She earned money in two different ways. She helped pick cotton, and she washed and ironed clothes, both very hard jobs. When she finally earned enough money, she attended the Colored Agricultural and Normal University (Langston University today). Unfortunately, she had to drop out after she ran out of money.

Bessie didn't want to go back to what she used to do and knew there were more opportunities up North. In 1915, she moved to Chicago and attended the Burnham School of Beauty Culture. She found a job at a local barbershop, and she began working as a **manicurist**, a person who treats and takes care of hands and fingernails.

During this time in Bessie's life, World War I had started. Bessie lived in her brothers' home while they served in the United States military. Bessie was fascinated by her brothers' stories about their time in France, especially about women who could fly airplanes. This was when she began to have the desire to learn how to fly. Unfortunately, none of the flight schools would let her attend because she was African American and a woman.

Bessie took a big step and left the United States. She moved to France. In 1922, Bessie Coleman received her air pilot's license from the Federation Aeronautique Internationale in France and had her first public flight. She became the first African American and Native American woman to become a pilot.

Over the next few years, Bessie performed at flight shows, gave flight lessons and went around the world doing speeches. Bessie would often refuse to go to segregated places. **Segregation** is setting one group of people apart from another group. Most of the time, one group was treated unfairly. Bessie was deeply admired for standing up for things that were wrong.

Bessie had plans to open an aviation school. Unfortunately, on April 30, 1926, she lost her life during an exhibition in Jacksonville, Florida. She always encouraged other African Americans and women to learn how to fly. There are many who were inspired by "Queen Bess."

Bessie had to travel all the way to France to get her pilot's license. Can you find France on a

map? Where would you like to travel to someday?

JANET HARMON BRAGG

1907-1993

Janet Harmon Bragg is one of the first African American female pilots to hold a commercial pilot's license.

Janet Harmon Bragg was born in 1907 in Griffin, Georgia. She attended Spelman College in

Atlanta, where she earned a nursing degree. After graduation, Janet moved to Chicago to work as a registered nurse. Inspired by Bessie Coleman, Janet had always wanted to learn how to fly. Like Bessie, Janet also had a hard time obtaining her pilot license because she was an African American woman. Janet wouldn't have to leave the United States to earn the license.

In 1932, she enrolled in the Curtiss–Wright Aeronautical University (CWAU). The school started out as being only for whites, but when Cornelius Coffey and John C. Robinson threatened to sue the school, **segregated** classes were offered. Coffey and Robinson were the first African American graduates from CWAU and later became instructors.

Despite this new opportunity for African Americans, Janet still faced issues because she was the only woman who enrolled. Being the only female was hard, and Janet didn't receive respect. Janet decided to use funds from her job as a nurse to purchase an airplane. This earned her some respect since her purchase helped other flight school students. She earned her private pilot license in 1934 and later became an instructor for CWAU.

Despite having a pilot license, Janet was still not allowed to use her skills. During World War II, Janet was encouraged by one of her white female students to apply for the Women's Airforce Service Pilots (WASP) Organization. WASP representatives were surprised to see Janet was "colored" and decided not to pursue the interview with her. Despite being a registered nurse for years, Janet was not even accepted into the military nurse corps.

The **Tuskegee Airmen** were African American servicemen who trained at the Tuskegee Army Air Field in Alabama during World War II. Janet enrolled in the Civilian Pilot Training Program at Tuskegee Institute to earn her commercial pilot's license. Even though she took the courses and passed the written test, Janet did not receive a license after her flight test. Not discouraged, Janet returned to Chicago and retook the test, finally earning her commercial pilot's license. **Commercial** pilots are paid to fly and can transport passengers or cargo.

Janet helped form the National Association of American Airmen, an organization that encouraged other African American men or women to learn how to fly. While she retired from flying in 1965, Janet continued to support others in aviation until her death in 1993. She'd clocked in around 2,000 flight hours.

Like Bessie Coleman, Janet opened doors for future female pilots. Our next pilot followed behind Janet a few years later.

Janet was inspired to learn how to fly from watching Bessie Coleman's achievements. Is there someone who inspires you?

WILLA B. BROWN

1906-1992

Willa B. Brown is one of the first African-American woman in the U.S. to earn a commercial pilot's license.

Willa Beatrice Brown was born in Glasglow, Kentucky. The former teacher moved to Chicago to become a social worker. During her time in Chicago, she also discovered she wanted to learn how to fly. Only a few years after Janet Harmon Bragg was a student, Willa enrolled in Curtiss Wright Aeronautical University (CWAU).

Willa earned her private pilot license in 1937. Two years later, Willa became the first African-American woman in the U.S. to earn a **commercial** pilot's license. In 1943, she became the first woman in the U.S. to have a mechanic's license and a commercial pilot's license. She learned how to fly planes and worked on fixing them too.

Willa married her former flight instructor, Cornelius Coffey. Together, the couple founded the Cornelius Coffey School of Aeronautics. Their school became the first African American owned private flight training academy in the United States. Before the school closed in 1945, it was known for training many of the men who served as **Tuskegee Airmen** during World War II.

In 1946, Willa's had achievements outside of aviation, like becoming the first African American woman to run for Congress. She didn't succeed in the election, but she was recognized for her efforts.

Trivia Question: These female pilots have a lot in common. Did you notice that they all moved to the same city? What's the name of the city?

You can find the answer in the "**More Women to Know**" section at the end of this chapter.

TIMELINE

1922

Bessie Coleman received her air pilot's license from the Federation Aeronautique Internationale in France and had her first public flight.

1934

Janet Harmon Bragg earned her private pilot license.

1939

Willa B. Brown became the first African American woman in the U.S. to hold a commercial pilot's license.

1942

Janet Harmon Bragg obtained her commercial pilot's license.

1943

Willa B. Brown became the first woman in the U.S. to have a mechanic's license and a commercial pilot's license.

1972

Willa B. Brown- Chappelle was appointed to the Federal Aviation Administration's (FAA) Women's Advisory Board.

MORE WOMEN TO KNOW!

1981 - Theresa Claiborne became the first African-American female pilot in the U.S. Air Force. Currently, she's also one of two African American female captains at United Airlines.

1995 - Melissa "M'Lis" Ward, a United Airlines pilot, is the first African-American female *captain* in commercial passenger aviation.

2000 - Lt. Col. Shawna Rochelle Kimbrell is the first female African American fighter pilot in the history of the U.S. Air Force.

2005 - Jeanine McIntosh-Menze became the first African American woman pilot in the U.S. Coast Guard.

2010 - La'Shanda Holmes became the first African American female helicopter pilot for the Coast Guard.

2017 - Captain Tara Wright is also the first African American female pilot to become a captain at Alaska Airline. In 2018, **Captain Wright** and **First Officer Mallory Cav**e piloted a flight from San Francisco to Portland, making them the first African American female crew for a U.S. airline.

2020 - Lt. j.g. Madeline Swegle became the U.S. Navy's first Black female tactical fighter pilot.

2021 - Captain Tahira Brown and **First Officer Diana Lugemwa** became the first African American female crew to fly a FedEx aircraft.

For more information about the women mentioned, find web links at https://thekulturekidz.com/more-women-to-know-aviation/

Trivia Question Answer: Chicago

Astronauts & Engineers

An **engineer** can design or build some pretty complex things like machines, systems, or structures. In order to become an engineer, attending college is required. When you attend a four-year college, the first degree you earn is a bachelor's degree. You can continue going to school by attending graduate school, with the next degree being a masters. When a person receives a Ph.D., that's the highest degree you can receive from a college or university.

In this section, you will meet three African American women who are engineers. Their career paths are all different, with two of them being astronauts.

These are some acronyms that you will see quite a few times.

NASA - National Aeronautics and Space Administration

GSFC - Goddard Space Flight Center

DR. MAE C. JEMISON

1956-

Dr. Mae C. Jemison, an engineer and a physician, is the first African American female astronaut.

Mae C. Jemison was born in Decatur, Alabama. She is the youngest of three children. As a young girl, Mae spent a lot of time reading and found herself drawn to learning more about astronomy. **Astronomy** is the study of everything in the universe, like planets, stars, comets, and galaxies.

In 1973, after she graduated from high school, she went to Stanford University on a National Achievement Scholarship. In 1977, she graduated from Stanford University with a degree in chemical engineering. A **chemical engineer** creates and designs processes using chemicals. They often work in a laboratory.

Dr. Jemison later earned a medical degree from Cornell University. During her time working as a doctor in Los Angeles, California, NASA selected her and fourteen others for astronaut training. Dr. Jemison completed her training as a mission specialist with NASA in 1988. She became the first African American female astronaut in 1992 on the Space Shuttle *Endeavor*.

The part of the space shuttle that carried astronauts is known as an orbiter or a spaceplane. Six orbiters were built for flight: *Enterprise, Columbia, Challenger, Discovery, Atlantis,* and *Endeavour*. The *Endeavor* was the final orbiter. It was built to replace the *Challenger*, which tragically exploded 73 seconds into its flight, killing the seven crew members on January 28, 1986.

After her historic space flight, Dr. Jemison resigned from NASA in 1993 and founded the Jemison Group, Inc. Among her current projects are several that focus on improving healthcare in Africa. Dr. Jemison worked as a professor of environmental studies at Dartmouth College from 1995 to 2002.

She continues to encourage children to pursue careers in science and has written children's books.

Dr. Jemison had two careers in STEM. One as a physician and the other as an astronaut. If you could work in two different STEM careers, what would they be?

STEPHANIE D. WILSON

1966-

Stephanie D. Wilson is the second African American woman to go into space after Mae

Jemison. She's flown to space onboard three Space Shuttle missions.

Stephanie Denise Wilson was born in Boston, Massachusetts, in 1966. Stephanie's parents exposed her to the world of engineering. Her dad was an **electrical engineer**, a career involving studying and designing devices, equipment, and systems that use electricity. Her mother worked at Lockheed Martin, a global security and aerospace company.

It was during middle school that Stephanie really learned what she wanted to do when she grew up. She had a chance to interview an **astronomer**, a person who studies everything in the universe like planets, stars, comets, and galaxies.

Stephanie's interest in space grew as she began her journey after graduating from high school. In 1988, she earned a bachelor's degree in engineering science from Harvard University. After graduation, she worked as an engineer for Martin Marietta Astronautics Group in Denver, Colorado. Stephanie decided to return to school and work on her master's degree. In 1992, armed with a master's degree in aerospace engineering, Stephanie began working at the Jet Propulsion Laboratory in Pasadena, California.

Finally, in April 1996, Stephanie's dream of becoming an astronaut became a reality. She was one of 43 people selected to be an astronaut candidate. There were over 2,500 people who applied! As an astronaut candidate, Stephanie had to train for being inside a space shuttle. Her training took place at the Johnson Space Center, where Stephanie would eventually become a Mission Specialist.

On July 4, 2006, Stephanie made her first journey into space on the Space Shuttle *Discovery*. This was about 14 years after Mae C. Jemison became the first African American female astronaut in space. As of 2021, Stephanie has logged 42 days in space, the most of any female African American astronaut.

In 2020, Stephanie became one of 18 astronauts training for the NASA Artemis program. This program is planning to send the first woman and the next man to the moon. On July 21, 1969, Neil Armstrong became the first person to walk on the moon. Stephanie could possible be the first woman to walk on the moon.

Did you know Stephanie brings mementos or something special as a reminder from her hometown and former schools while she goes up in space? If you went up in space, what would you bring with you?

DR. APRILLE ERICSSON-JACKSON

1963 -

Aprille Ericsson-Jackson, an aerospace engineer, is the first African American woman to earn PhDs in Mechanical Engineering from two institutions.

Aprille Ericsson-Jackson was born in Brooklyn, New York and has three younger sisters. While she was in school, she learned that she loved science and mathematics. Graduating from high school with high honors, Aprille moved forward to begin her career in engineering.

She earned her first degree, a Bachelor of Science in Aeronautical and Astronautical Engineering, at Massachusetts Institute of Technology (also known as MIT) in 1986. Aprille went on to earn a Master of Engineering from Howard University in 1992. She became the first African American woman to receive a Ph.D. in Mechanical Engineering from Howard University in 1995.

Mechanical engineers study how things work and design solutions for making things work better. Dr. Ericsson-Jackson earned a second Ph.D. in Mechanical Engineering from NASA GSFC, making her the first African American female to have two PhDs in Mechanical engineering.

In 2003, Dr. Ericsson-Jackson began working at the NASA GSFC as an aerospace engineer. **Aerospace** is the study of the earth's atmosphere and space. With aerospace and mechanical engineering as her background, what do you think were some of the things Dr. Ericsson-Jackson did at her job?

First, let's learn some vocabulary words. A **satellite** can be a moon, planet or object that **orbit** or moves along a curved path around another planet or a star. The moon is known as a natural satellite, and it orbits around the earth. The Earth orbits around the sun, which is the largest star in our universe. NASA has artificial satellites that they launched in space to help with communication here on earth.

When Dr. Ericsson-Jackson started working at NASA GSFC, her job title was altitude control systems analyst. In this job, she made sure the satellites that orbit the earth and beyond followed the correct trajectory or path.

Today, Dr. Ericsson-Jackson continues to work at NASA GSFC as the New Business Lead in Instrument Systems and Technology Division.

After reading about these three engineers, are you interested in learning more about space? At the end of this chapter, are more women to know.

TIMELINE

1988

Dr. Mae C. Jemison completed her training as a mission specialist with NASA.

1992

Dr. Mae C. Jemison became the first African American female astronaut when she flew on the Space Shuttle *Endeavor*.

1995

Dr. Aprille Ericsson-Jackson became the first African-American woman to receive a Ph.D. in Mechanical Engineering from Howard University.

2006

Stephanie D. Wilson made her first journey into space on the Space Shuttle *Discovery*, becoming the second African American female astronaut.

2020

Stephanie D. Wilson became one of 18 astronauts training for the NASA Artemis program. She could be the first woman to walk on the moon.

MORE WOMEN TO KNOW!

2008 - Joan Higginbotham, a NASA astronaut and an electrical engineer, is the third African American woman to go into space, after Mae C. Jemison and Stephanie D. Wilson.

2013 - Aisha Bowe, an aerospace engineer and a former NASA rocket scientist founded STEMBoard.

2021 - Dr. Sian Proctor was launched into Earth orbit, on September 15, 2021, as the pilot of the Crew Dragon space capsule, making her the first African American woman to pilot a spacecraft.

2022 - Jessica Andrea Watkins, a NASA astronaut and geologist, is the first Black woman to complete an International Space Station long-term mission.

For more information about the women mentioned, find web links at <u>https://thekulturekidz.com/more-women-to-know-aviation/</u>

PART 2
COMPUTER SCIENCE

Part 2: Computer Science

Human Computers

Before personal computers became popular, there were people known as **human computers** or research mathematicians. They were really, really good with math and asked to solve complex problems.

One place where human computers were needed was at NASA. In the previous chapter, you learned about astronauts and engineers who worked at

NASA. During the early years of NASA (back then called NACA), there were several African American women who helped with the success of the space program. Let's meet some of them.

What Do These Mean?

These are some acronyms that you will see quite a few times.

NACA - National Advisory Committee for Aeronautics

NASA - National Aeronautics and Space Administration

MARY JACKSON

1921-2005

Mary Winston Jackson was an American mathematician and aerospace engineer at NASA.

Mary Winston was born on April 9, 1921, in Hampton, Virginia. She excelled in school and graduated with honors from George P. Phenix Training School.

In 1942, Mary earned a bachelor's degree in mathematics and physical science from Hampton Institute (now Hampton University). After she graduated, Mary taught math for a year before becoming a bookkeeper at the National Catholic Community Center. In 1951, Mary was recruited by NACA and worked as a "human computer" at Langley Research Center in Hampton, Virginia. She would work beside other women like Katherine Jackson and Dorothy Vaughan, her supervisor, in the West Area Computing Unit. Even though the African American women in this unit helped with the complex math problems, they had to be **segregated** from the white workers. That meant they worked in separate areas and used separate bathrooms and cafeterias.

In 1953, Mary began working for a NASA engineer named Kazimierz Czarnecki. She worked on the Supersonic Pressure Tunnel, which was a wind tunnel. Engineers would create winds almost at the speed of sound (super fast!) and study how the forces (the push or pull) affected the model inside the wind tunnel. Her boss, Czarnecki, thought

Mary would make a great engineer. After some difficulties, Mary was finally allowed to take graduate-level math and physics courses at The University of Virginia. She obtained her degree in aerospace engineering and became NASA's first African American engineer in 1958.

Mary continued to work as an engineer at NASA until she retired in 1985.

Mary Jackson was featured in the movie, *Hidden Figures* in 2016. She was played by actress and singer Janelle Monáe.

KATHERINE JOHNSON

1918-2020

Katherine Johnson, a mathematician, is known as one of the first African-American women to work as a NASA scientist.

Katherine Johnson was born on August 26, 1918, in White Sulphur Springs, West Virginia. Her teachers noticed she had very strong math skills. When she was ten years old, Katherine's family enrolled her in a special high school. The school was located on the West Virginia State College campus.

When Katherine graduated from high school, she began attending West Virginia State. In 1937, Katherine graduated with degrees in mathematics and French. She was only eighteen years old.

She taught math for a few years before hearing about an opportunity with the National Advisory Committee for Aeronautics (NACA). They were hiring African American mathematicians. Katherine officially began working in 1953 alongside other women like Mary Jackson and Dorothy Vaughan. She worked in the West Computing Unit until 1958, when NASA replaced NACA.

After 1958, Katherine worked at NASA as an aerospace technologist. She became very good at calculating the **trajectory** or path needed for an orbital flight. On May 5, 1961, Alan Shepard would become the first American in space thanks to Katherine's calculations. During her career, she also provided calculations to help with the Apollo Moon landing and the start of the Space Shuttle program.

Katherine retired from NASA in 1986, but her role and legacy became more widely known after the *Hidden Figures* movie was released in 2016. Actress Taraji P. Henson played Katherine.

She passed away at the age of 101 on February 24, 2020.

DOROTHY VAUGHAN

1910-2008

Dorothy Vaughan was a mathematician and NASA's first African-American manager.

Dorothy Vaughan was born September 20, 1910, in Kansas City, Missouri. Her family moved to West Virginia when Dorothy was seven years old. An excellent student throughout school, Dorothy graduated as class valedictorian, the top student in her entire class.

In 1929, she graduated from Wilberforce University with a bachelor of arts degree in mathematics. She started her career as a math teacher. There weren't a lot of jobs that an African American could work during her time, but things began to change. NACA needed a lot of mathematicians, also known as "human computers." Dorothy stopped being a teacher and began working at Langley Memorial Aeronautical Laboratory in 1943.

She and her co-workers, Katherine Johnson and Mary Jackson, worked together in the West Computing Unit. Dorothy received a promotion in 1949, becoming the first African American manager at NASA. As a supervisor, Dorothy stood up for her fellow female "human computers" and gained the trust of many of the white employees. She would manage West Computing for almost ten years until the division was shut down by NASA.

She remained working at NASA until 1971.

In 2016, Dorothy Vaughan was also featured in the movie, *Hidden Figures*. Actress Octavia Spencer played Dorothy.

These three human computers were among many women who were "hidden" behind the scenes. Only recently have we learned about their role in the Space Race. How do you think you would feel being in their shoes?

TIMELINE

1943

The NACA West Computing Unit started with a group of female African American mathematicians who worked as "human computers."

1949

Dorothy Vaughan became the first African American manager at NASA.

1958

The NACA West Computing Unit ended.

1958

Mary Jackson obtained her degree in aerospace engineering and became NASA's first African American engineer.

1961

On May 5, 1961, Alan Shepard would become the first American in space thanks to **Katherine Johnson's** calculations.

MORE WOMEN TO KNOW!

1959 - **Melba Roy Mouton** started working for NASA. During the 1960s she was Assistant Chief of Research Programs at NASA's Trajectory and Geodynamics Division and headed the group of NASA mathematicians called "computers" (included Mary Jackson, Katherine Johnson and Dorothy Vaughan).

1967 - **Christine Darden** started her career at NASA as a human computer too. She later became one of the few African American female aerospace engineers. Her main assignment was creating a computer program for sonic boom. A sonic boom is caused when an object moves faster than the speed of sound, making a really loud sound similar to thunder.

For more information about the women mentioned, find web links at https://thekulturekidz.com/more-women-to-know-computer-science/

Technology

What do you think about when you hear the word "technology?" You may think about a smartphone, tablet or computer. It can also be other things like video games, electric cars, social media or even the artificial intelligence voice (like Alexa, Siri, etc.) that answers you back when you ask a question.

MARSHA RHEA WILLIAMS

1948-

Dr. Marsha Rhea Williams is the first African American woman to earn a Ph.D. in computer science.

Marsha Rhea Williams was born in Memphis, Tennessee. Marsha was a gifted student who had a love for math and science. She earned a bachelor's degree in physics from Beloit College in 1969. She continued her education at the University of Michigan and earned a master's degree in physics. In 1982, Marsha became the first African American woman to earn a PhD in computer science from Vanderbilt University.

It was rare to see an African American female professor in Computer Science. Marsha taught at Memphis State College, Fisk University, the University of Mississippi in Oxford and Tennessee State University.

Today, she still teaches at Tennessee State University, where she is a tenured professor. **Tenure** means a person has a job, usually at a college or university, for the rest of their life. They cannot be fired without a very good reason.

Are you interested in computers? Do you want to learn how to code?

MARIAN ROGERS CROAK

1955 -

Marian Rogers Croak has created many inventions, including Voice over Internet Protocol (VoIP) and donating by text messaging.

Marian Rogers Croak attended Princeton University for her undergraduate studies. In 1982, she earned her **doctorate** from the University of Southern California. A doctorate is the highest degree a student can earn from a college or university. Marian focused on two areas, statistical analysis and social psychology. Statistical analysis is the science of collecting and exploring large amounts of data to find out if there are any patterns or trends. Social psychology is the science of studying how a person or a group of people's behavior may be affected by others.

You're probably thinking, how did Marian use her studies in her career. Not too long after she graduated in 1982, Marian began working at AT&T in a department called the Human Factors Division. Her job was to figure out how technology could help people.

It was during this time that Marian invented **Voice over Internet Protocol** or **VoIP**. VoIP is a type of technology that allows a person to talk on a phone using the internet. Later, Marian created a way for people to donate money to charities by using text messaging on the phone. In 2005 when Hurricane Katrina hit New Orleans, her invention helped people all over donate money easily to help the victims.

Marian has over 200 patents and loves encouraging young girls to pursue STEM careers. She is one of two African American women inducted into the National Inventors Hall of Fame. You will meet the other woman later in this book.

Can you think of an invention that would help people?

LISA GELOBTER

1971-

Lisa Gelobter is a computer scientist and entrepreneur who played a role in creating many internet technologies.

Lisa Gelobter graduated from Brown University in 1991 with a computer science degree, her concentration in **artificial intelligence** and machine learning. Artificial intelligence, also known as AI, is when a computer or robot has been programmed to perform tasks that are usually done by people.

For over twenty-five years, Lisa has worked on many internet technologies. One is Shockwave, a plugin that helps people view animations, play video games or watch videos online. She also helped create Hulu, a popular streaming service for watching television shows and movies.

You may have heard the word "digital" before. **Digital** includes all types of technologies like social media, online games, videos, podcasts and websites. Lisa has worked as the Chief Digital Officer for BET Networks. In 2015, President Barack Obama asked Lisa to join the United States Digital Service. This department uses design and technology to bring services to Americans. Later, she served as the Chief Digital Service Officer for the Department of Education.

Also, an entrepreneur, Lisa currently is the Chief Executive Officer of her company, tEQuitable. Founded in 2017, the company's mission is to stop discrimination and harassment in the workplace. **Discrimination** is when people are treated differently and usually not in a very nice way. **Harassment** is when a person annoys or makes someone upset over and over again.

You may have used some of the technologies that Lisa worked on. Do you play video games online?

TIMELINE

1982

Marsha Rhea Williams becomes the first African American woman to earn a PhD in computer science.

2005

When Hurricane Katrina hit New Orleans, **Marian Rogers Croak's** invention helped people all over donate money using text messaging.

2015

President Barack Obama asked **Lisa Gelobter** to join the United States Digital Service.

2017

Lisa Gelobter founded her company, tEQuitable.

MORE WOMEN TO KNOW!

1987 - Carol Yvonne Espy-Wilson, an electrical engineer, received her Ph.D. in Electrical Engineering from the Massachusetts Institute of Technology (MIT), becoming the first African-American woman to earn this degree from MIT.

2009 - Ursula M. Burns was the CEO of Xerox from 2009 to 2016, the first African American woman to serve as CEO of a Fortune 500 company.

2011 - **Kimberly Bryant**, an electrical engineer, founded Black Girls Code after her daughter expressed an interest in learning computer programming.

2021 - **Ayanna MacCalla Howard**, an American roboticist, entrepreneur and educator, became the dean of the College of Engineering at Ohio State University, making her the first woman to lead the Ohio State College of Engineering.

2021 - Window **Snyder**, a computer security expert, founded her company, Thistle Technologies. She became one of the first computer scientists to specialize in cyber security and has worked at major technology companies like Apple, Microsoft, Intel and Mozilla.

For more information about the women mentioned, find web links at https://thekulturekidz.com/more-women-to-know-computer-science/

PART 3
HEALTH SCIENCE

Part 3: Health Science

Pioneers

Did you know healthcare is the largest and fastest-growing industry in the United States?

There are many different health science careers. You can be a physician, surgeon, nurse, dentist, medical lab technician, researcher, therapist, chemist, and so much more.

In the next few pages, you will meet African American females who were firsts in their field.

MARY ELIZA MAHONEY, RN

1845 – 1926

Mary Eliza Mahoney was the first African American registered nurse in the United States.

Mary Eliza Mahoney was born in 1845 in Boston, Massachusetts. Her parents were freed slaves. She had a dream of becoming a nurse. When she was a teenager, she started working at the New England Hospital for Women and Children. Mary worked as a janitor, cook, washerwoman and a nurse's aide before her dream was fulfilled.

At the age of 33, Mary finally enrolled in the New England Hospital for Women and Children Nursing School in 1878. The nursing program was a lot of work. Out of the 18 trainees who enrolled, nine continued with the program. Mary was one of the four to complete the program in 1879, making her the first African American registered nurse in the United States.

Even though Mary was a registered nurse, she still experienced discrimination. Most of her career was as a private nurse where she could provide care to individuals. She received patients from wealthy white families and was known for how well she cared for her patients.

In 1908, Mary co-founded the National Association of Colored Graduate Nurses (NACGN) and gave the opening speech at the NACGN first convention.

In later years, Mary was an active participant in the Women's Suffrage Movement. When the 19th

Amendment was passed, she was one of the first African American women in Boston to register to vote.

Sometimes when you are younger, you have an idea about what you want to do. That's how it was for Mary. What about you? Have you thought about what you want to do when you get older?

DR. SUSAN MCKINNEY STEWARD

1847 – 1918

Dr. Susan McKinney Steward was the first African American woman physician in New York and the third African American woman physician in the U.S.

In 1847, **Dr. Susan McKinney Steward** was born in Brooklyn, New York. She was the seventh of ten children. Susan's parents were wealthy pork farmers, and they made sure all their children received an education. Susan's sisters were public school principals, teachers and piano players.

Susan graduated from the New York Medical School for Women and Children as valedictorian of her class in 1870. She became the first African American woman physician in New York and the third African American woman physician in the United States. Even though Dr. McKinney had excelled at medical school, she wasn't always welcome at Bellevue Hospital during her **residency**. A residency is when a doctor is learning to become better and better at their specialty.

Despite the obstacles she faced due to the color of her skin, Dr. McKinney specialized in prenatal care and childhood **diseases** or sicknesses. When she opened her private practice, Dr. McKinney became known for her care and treatment of malnutrition in children. **Malnutrition** is caused when a person does not get the right amount of nutrients to help them live and, for children, grow.

Dr. McKinney had a successful private practice in Brooklyn for more than 20 years before getting married for a second time. Her new husband,

Theophilus Gould Steward, was a US Army chaplain. Because her husband was in the military, Dr. McKinney Steward traveled with him. She earned medical licenses in Montana and Wyoming.

In 1898, Dr. McKinney Steward began working as a physician and taught at Wilberforce University in Ohio. She remained at Wilberforce until her death in 1918.

Dr. Susan McKinney Steward, like many doctors, chose the healthcare of children as her specialty. If you become a doctor, what would be your specialty?

DR. IDA GRAY NELSON ROLLINS

1866-1953

Dr. Ida Gray Nelson Rollins was the first African American woman to earn a Doctor of Dental Surgery degree.

Ida Gray was born in Tennessee in 1867. When she was a teenager, her mother died, and Ida went to live with her aunt in Ohio. She found work as a seamstress and dressmaker before getting a job at Jonathan Taft's dental office.

Taft was the first dean of the dental college at the University of Michigan, and he encouraged women to enroll in the program. With her mentor's encouragement, Ida graduated in 1890 and became the first African American woman to earn a Doctor of Dental Surgery degree.

Ida ran a successful private practice in Cincinnati before marrying her first husband, James S. Nelson. They moved to Chicago, where Dr. Ida Gray became the first African American, male or female, to practice dentistry in Chicago.

She would continue to practice as a dentist in Chicago for the remainder of her life.

A dentist will help ensure you are taking good care of your teeth. Have you been to the dentist lately?

DR. ELLA PHILLIPS STEWART

1893 – 1987

Dr. Ella Phillips Stewart was the first African American to graduate and become the first African American woman to pass the Pennsylvania State Board Pharmacology Exam.

Ella Phillips Stewart was born on March 6, 1893, in Stringtown, West Virginia. She was the daughter of sharecroppers. Ella planned to become a teacher but began working at a pharmacy as a **bookkeeper**, a person who helps a business manage its finances. She soon became interested in **pharmacology** which is the study of how drugs, both chemical and natural, affect living organisms.

Determined to become a pharmacist, she applied to the University of Pittsburgh (also known as Pitt) School of Pharmacy. Her application was rejected, but that didn't stop Ella. After much persistence, she enrolled in the program, but it wasn't easy being an African American on the campus.

In 1916, Ella graduated from Pitt's School of Pharmacy, becoming the first African American woman to graduate from this program. Later, she became the first African American woman to pass the Pennsylvania State Board Pharmacology Exam.

After earning her degree, she worked at a drug store owned by two of her fellow Pitt classmates. She eventually opened her own drug store, Myers Pharmacy, in Pittsburg.

In 1920, Ella married William Wyatt Stewart, who was also a pharmacist. The couple worked in a variety of drug stores before opening their own business in Toledo, Ohio. Stewart's Pharmacy was established in July 1922.

Ella and William lived above the pharmacy and often had well-known African Americans visit, like Marian Anderson, Mary McLeod Bethune, and W. E. B. Du Bois. Stewart's Pharmacy remained open until 1945.

The pharmacist was also active in civic organizations like the National Association of Colored Women's Club. During the 1950s, Ella was appointed as a goodwill ambassador, and she represented the United States as she traveled in Asia.

When you get sick, a doctor will prescribe special medicine to help you feel better. Pharmacists help fill the doctor's prescriptions. Have you ever been to a pharmacy or had a special prescription?

TIMELINE

1870

Dr. Susan McKinney Steward graduated from the New York Medical School for Women and Children as valedictorian of her class. She became the first African American woman physician in New York and the third African American woman physician in the United States.

1879

Mary Eliza Mahoney became the first African American registered nurse in the United States.

1890

Dr. Ida Gray Nelson Rollins graduated and became the first African American woman to earn a Doctor of Dental Surgery degree.

1916

Ella Phillips Stewart graduated from Pitt's School of Pharmacy, becoming the first African American woman to graduate from this program. Later, she became the first African American woman to pass the Pennsylvania State Board Pharmacology Exam.

1922

Ella and her husband, William Wyatt Stewart, opened their own drug store, Stewart's Pharmacy, in Toledo, Ohio.

MORE WOMEN TO KNOW!

In 1864, **Rebecca Crumpler, MD,** was the first Black woman in the United States to earn an MD.

In 1867, **Rebecca Cole, MD,** became the second African-American woman to become a doctor in the United States.

Julia Pearl Hughes became one of the first black female hospital pharmacists when she went to work at the Frederick Douglas Memorial Hospital in Philadelphia. In 1899, she became the first African-American woman pharmacist to own and operate her own drug store, Hughes Pharmacy.

For more information about the women mentioned, find web links at https://thekulturekidz.com/more-women-to-know-health-science/

Modern Medicine

People are needed in health science to research new ways to help people. They often work in laboratories to study how the body reacts to illnesses, injuries, and physical ailments. It's during these studies, new medicine, new inventions and sometimes cures are achieved.

DR. MARIE M. DALY

1921–2003

Dr. Marie M. Daly is the first African American woman to receive a PhD in chemistry in the United States.

Dr. Marie Maynard Daly was born in Queens, New York. Marie's father was attending Cornell University, working on a bachelor's degree in chemistry, but he had to drop out. Marie picked up on her father's love for science.

After graduating from the all-female Hunter College High School, Marie enrolled in Queens College. She graduated magma cum laude in 1942 with a bachelor's degree in chemistry. A year later, she completed her master's degree.

Marie saved money by tutoring chemistry students and enrolled in the doctoral program at Columbia University. She focused on studying how compounds in the body affected digestion. A **compound** is formed when two or more different elements come together. Some elements found in the human body are oxygen, carbon, hydrogen, nitrogen, calcium, and phosphorus.

In 1947, Marie became the first African American woman to obtain a PhD in chemistry in the United States.

Dr. Daly taught at many higher education institutions like Howard University in Washington, DC, The Rockefeller University in New York, and Columbia University. She joined The Albert Einstein College of Medicine in 1960 and taught there until she retired in 1986.

Dr. Daly never forgot who inspired her love of science. She honored her father by creating a scholarship for African American science students who attended her alma mater Queens College.

Who inspires you? How can you honor them?

DR. PATRICIA BATH

1942-2019

Dr. Patricia Bath was the first African American resident in ophthalmology at New York University. She also was the first African American female doctor to secure a medical patent.

Dr. Patricia Bath was an **ophthalmologist**, a doctor who specializes in eye and vision care. As a young girl, she dreamed about becoming a doctor. She was an excellent student in school. In fact, by the time she was sixteen years old, Bath pursued her dream of becoming a doctor by attending Howard University College of Medicine in Washington, D.C. After graduating from medical school, Bath became an intern at Harlem Hospital in New York.

Interns, also known as first-year residents, are doctors. During their first year of practicing medicine, they have to be supervised while they are with patients. After the first year, the doctor begins a residency, which can last for 2-7 years. During the residency, the doctor is learning to become better and better at their specialty.

Dr. Bath's specialty during her residency was eye and vision care. She became the first African American resident in ophthalmology at New York University. During her residency, she noticed many of her patients were blind or visually impaired. Many of these patients were African Americans who had not been to see an eye doctor usually because they couldn't afford to go.

So passionate about eye care, Dr. Bath and three other colleagues founded the American Institute for the Prevention of Blindness (AIPB). The organization's goal was to make sure anyone, no matter their race or economic status had access to eye care.

She was also known as a laser scientist. A **laser** is an instrument that produces a powerful beam of light. With a lot of research, Dr. Bath invented the Laserphaco Probe, a tool that corrects cataracts during eye surgery. **Cataracts** are an eye condition that can lead to blindness, and Dr. Bath's tool provided a safe way to remove them.

When she patented the Laserphaco Probe in 1988, Bath became the first African American female doctor to secure a medical patent.

In an earlier chapter, you learned about Marian Rogers Croak being one of two African American women inducted into the National Inventors Hall of Fame. Dr. Bath was the other woman.

If you were a doctor, what would be your specialty?

TIMELINE

1947

Dr. Marie M. Daly became the first African American woman to obtain a PhD in chemistry in the United States.

1988

Dr. Patricia Bath became the first African American female doctor to secure a medical patent for her Laserphaco Probe.

MORE WOMEN TO KNOW!

In 1948-49, **Dorothy Lavinia Brown, MD,** became the first Black woman surgeon in the South.

In 1993, **Barbara Ross-Lee, DO,** became the first Black woman to be appointed dean of a US medical school. She remained dean of the College of Osteopathic Medicine of Ohio University until 2001.

In 1981, **Alexa Irene Canady, MD,** became the first Black woman to become a neurosurgeon in the United States.

In 1993, **Dr. Joycelyn Elders** was the first African American and only the second woman to head the U.S. Public Health Service.

For more information about the women mentioned, find web links at https://thekulturekidz.com/more-women-to-know-health-science/

Glossary

Several vocabulary words were introduced throughout the book. Below you can find a review of definitions and also how to say the words out loud. Some of these are great words to know if you are ever in a spelling bee!

Aerospace (eh-row-spays) - The study of the earth's atmosphere and space.

Astronomy (uh-straa-nuh-mee) - The study of everything in the universe like planets, stars, comets, and galaxies.

Cataracts (ka-tr-akts) - An eye condition that can lead to blindness.

Commercial (kuh-mur-shl) - The buying and selling of goods or services.

Digital (di-juh-tl) - Includes all types of technologies like social media, online games, videos, podcasts and websites.

Discrimination (duh-skri-muh-nay-shn) - When people are treated differently and usually not in a very nice way.

Doctorate (daak-tr-uht) - The highest degree a student can earn from a college or university, which is usually a PhD.

Engineer (en-juh-neer) - A person who can design or build some pretty complex things like machines, systems, or structures.

Entrepreneur (aan-truh-pruh-noor) - A person who creates and runs their own business.

Harassment (hr-as-muhnt) - When a person annoys or makes someone upset over and over again.

Ophthalmologist (aaf-thuh-maa-luh-juhst) - A doctor who specializes in eye and vision care.

Patent (pa-tnt) - A government document that gives an inventor the right to be the only maker of a product for a certain number of years.

Satellite (sa-tuh-lite) - A body like the moon, planet or object that orbit or moves along a curved path around another planet or a star.

Segregation (seh·gruh·gay·shn) - Setting one group of people apart from another group. Most of the times one group was treated unfairly.

Sharecropping (shehr-kraa-puhng) - Farmers had to give the landowner a portion of their crop.

Tenure (ten-yr) - A person has a job, usually at a college or university, for the rest of their life. They cannot be fired without a very good reason.

Trajectory (truh-jek-tr-ee) - A path needed for an orbital flight.

Tuskegee (tuh-skee-gee) **Airmen** - African American servicemen who trained at the Tuskegee Army Air Field in Alabama during World War II.

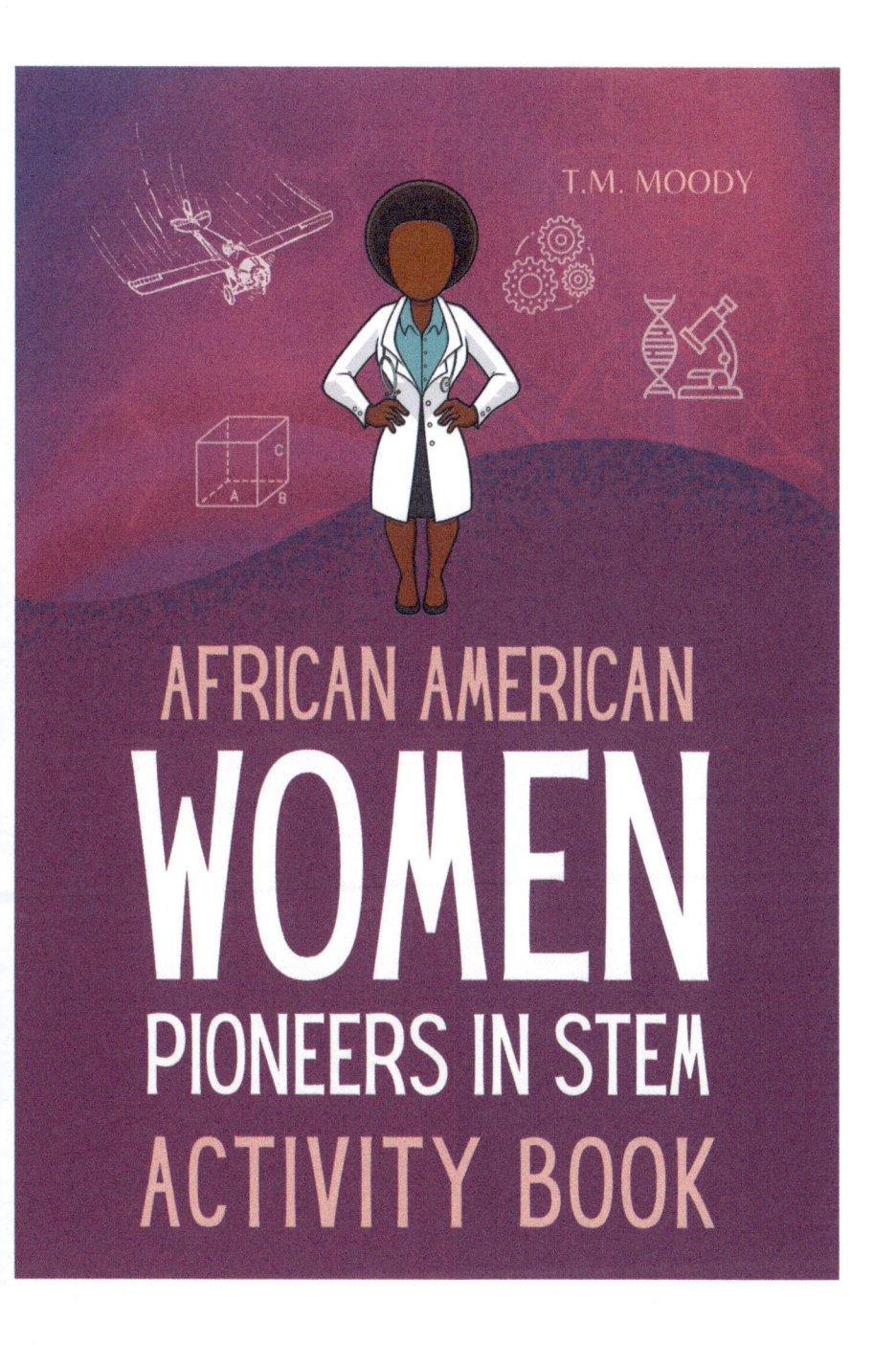

T.M. MOODY

AFRICAN AMERICAN
WOMEN
PIONEERS IN STEM
ACTIVITY BOOK

Activity Book

Do you like coloring or puzzles? Be sure to check out *African American Women Pioneers in STEM Activity Book*. The activity book includes over 45 activities like coloring, word search, crossword puzzles, mazes, and more. Download free puzzles at TheKultureKidz.com.

BLACK FEMALE PILOTS WORD SEARCH

Can you find all the hidden words?

```
I  A  N  A  E  L  E  A  I  I  E  T  E  N  N  T  A  I
A  E  A  C  U  U  R  S  I  I  C  I  U  M  O  E  T  V
E  R  T  E  X  G  I  O  H  E  H  G  N  H  A  I  I  T
E  O  A  L  S  L  E  G  T  G  N  F  L  I  G  H  T  I
G  N  N  A  P  F  N  S  P  I  E  M  R  M  G  A  I  H
E  A  V  I  A  T  I  O  N  I  I  P  E  E  O  S  I  U
K  U  M  T  I  L  K  I  M  E  L  E  L  C  N  T  N  E
S  T  I  U  R  I  A  I  I  A  C  O  H  H  G  E  E  C
U  I  E  E  E  R  N  L  N  E  E  I  T  A  A  T  E  R
T  C  O  T  T  S  O  E  G  A  I  I  L  N  I  F  E  A
E  S  G  E  R  G  I  R  H  C  I  E  I  I  E  E  T  S
C  N  E  X  H  I  B  I  T  I  O  N  N  C  I  I  N  T
E  A  M  V  S  H  S  E  G  R  E  G  A  T  I  O  N  K
I  P  C  P  M  E  P  A  T  I  N  L  O  U  O  A  S  S
M  I  O  N  T  I  L  U  N  N  T  I  E  S  R  I  E  E
S  C  P  R  I  L  A  I  C  R  E  M  M  O  C  A  A  U
A  O  E  S  A  A  I  A  S  E  A  E  I  A  N  E  E  L
L  S  N  L  S  L  P  E  H  E  L  L  I  L  I  F  I  O
```

WORD LIST

aeronautics	aviation	training	airplane
flight	pilot	license	commercial
exhibition	Tuskegee	segregation	mechanic

BLACK FEMALE PILOTS DOUBLE WORD PUZZLE

Did you notice all three pilots have something in common besides being women. Unscramble the words below to find out.

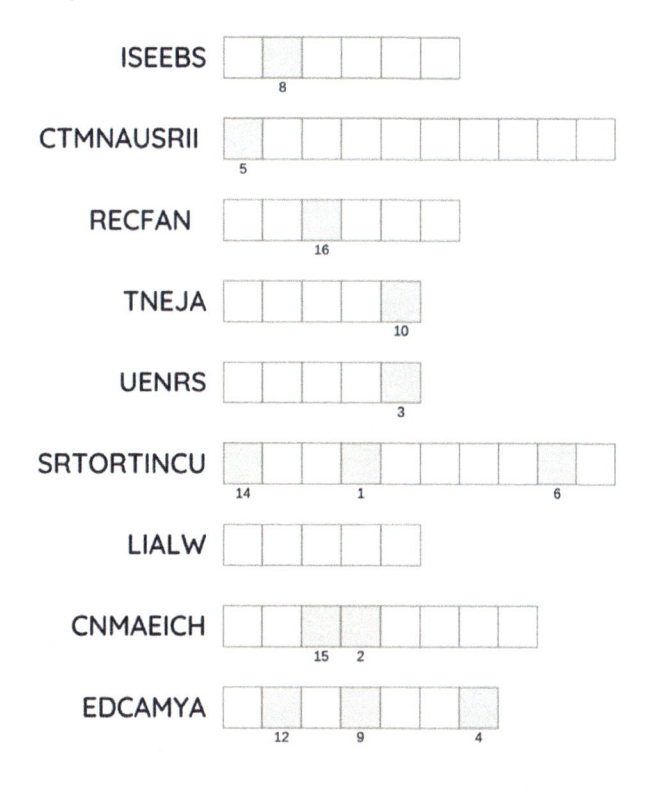

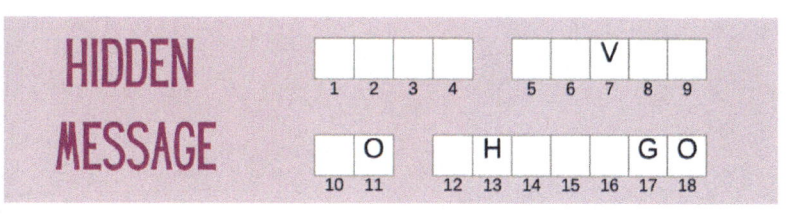

- ISEEBS ⬚⬚⬚⬚⬚⬚ (8)
- CTMNAUSRII ⬚⬚⬚⬚⬚⬚⬚⬚⬚⬚ (5)
- RECFAN ⬚⬚⬚⬚⬚⬚ (16)
- TNEJA ⬚⬚⬚⬚⬚ (10)
- UENRS ⬚⬚⬚⬚⬚ (3)
- SRTORTINCU ⬚⬚⬚⬚⬚⬚⬚⬚⬚⬚ (14, 1, 6)
- LIALW ⬚⬚⬚⬚⬚
- CNMAEICH ⬚⬚⬚⬚⬚⬚⬚⬚ (15, 2)
- EDCAMYA ⬚⬚⬚⬚⬚⬚⬚ (12, 9, 4)

HIDDEN MESSAGE

1	2	3	4	5	6	7	8	9
						V		

10	11	12	13	14	15	16	17	18
O		H					G	O

About the Author

T.M. Moody has a deep love for history and started the Kulture Kidz website in 1999. She has worked over twenty years as an education content creator and digital curator in public media. Her specialty is creating interactive, standards-based content for the K-12 community.

Moody also has been an author for over ten years. She writes mysteries under her real name, Tyora Moody.

Kulture Kidz Books

Kulture Kidz Books creates content and books for ages 6-12. Our mission is to learn about people who made a difference.

For this book's bibliography, visit https://thekulturekidz.com/bibliographies/

Made in the USA
Monee, IL
17 December 2022